A CALL

Grace MacGowan Cooke

[ZHINGOORA BOOKS]

This digital edition is published by Zhingoora Books.

The Cover is Designed by Pallav Sethiya.

zhingoora_books@yahoo.com

A CALL

Grace MacGowan Cooke

A boy in an unnaturally clean, country-laundered collar walked down a long white road. He scuffed the dust up wantonly, for he wished to veil the all-too-brilliant polish of his cowhide shoes. Also the memory of the whiteness and slipperiness of his collar oppressed him. He was fain to look like one accustomed to social diversions, a man hurried from hall to hall of pleasure, without time between to change collar or polish boot. He stooped and rubbed a crumb of earth on his overfresh neck-linen.

This did not long sustain his drooping spirit. He was mentally adrift upon the *Hints and Helps to Young Men in Business and Social Relations*, which had suggested to him his present enterprise, when the appearance of a second youth, taller and broader than himself, with a shock of light curling hair and a crop of freckles that advertised a rich soil threw him a lifeline. He put his thumbs to his lips and whistled in a peculiarly ear-splitting way. The two boys had sat on the same bench at Sunday-school not three hours before; yet what a change had come over the world for one of them since then!

"Hello! Where you goin', Ab?" asked the newcomer, gruffly.

"Callin'," replied the boy in the collar, laconically, but with carefully averted gaze.

"On the girls?" inquired the other, awestruck. In Mount Pisgah you saw the girls home from night church, socials, or parties; you could hang over the gate; and you might walk with a girl in the cemetery of a Sunday afternoon; but to ring a front-door bell and ask for Miss Heart's Desire one must have been in long trousers at least three years—and the two boys confronted in the dusty road had worn these dignifying garments barely six months.

"Girls," said Abner, loftily; "I don't know about girls— I'm just going to call on one girl—Champe Claiborne." He marched on as though the conversation was at an end; but Ross hung upon his flank. Ross and Champe were neighbors, comrades in all sorts of mischief; he was in doubt whether to halt Abner and pummel him, or propose to enlist under his banner.

"Do you reckon you could?" he debated, trotting along by the irresponsive Jilton boy.

"Run home to your mother," growled the originator of the plan, savagely. "You ain't old enough to call on girls; anybody can see that; but I am, and I'm going to call on Champe Claiborne."

Again the name acted as a spur on Ross. "With your collar and boots all dirty?" he jeered. "They won't know you're callin'."

4

The boy in the road stopped short in his dusty tracks. He was an intense creature, and he whitened at the tragic insinuation, longing for the wholesome stay and companionship of freckle-faced Ross. "I put the dirt on o' purpose so's to look kind of careless," he half whispered, in an agony of doubt. "S'pose I'd better go into your house and try to wash it off? Reckon your mother would let me?"

"I've got two clean collars," announced the other boy, proudly generous. "I'll lend you one. You can put it on while I'm getting ready. I'll tell mother that we're just stepping out to do a little calling on the girls."

Here was an ally worthy of the cause. Abner welcomed him, in spite of certain jealous twinges. He reflected with satisfaction that there were two Claiborne girls, and though Alicia was so stiff and prim that no boy would ever think of calling on her, there was still the hope that she might draw Ross's fire, and leave him, Abner, to make the numerous remarks he had stored up in his mind from *Hints and Helps to Young Men in Social and Business Relations* to Champe alone.

Mrs. Pryor received them with the easy-going kindness of the mother of one son. She followed them into the dining-room to kiss and feed him, with an absent "Howdy, Abner; how's your mother?"

Abner, big with the importance of their mutual intention, inclined his head stiffly and looked toward Ross for explanation. He trembled a little, but it was with delight, as he anticipated the effect of the speech Ross had outlined. But it did not come.

"I'm not hungry, mother," was the revised edition which the freckle-faced boy offered to the maternal ear. "I—we are going over to Mr. Claiborne's—on—er—on an errand for Abner's father."

The black-eyed boy looked reproach as they clattered up the stairs to Ross's room, where the clean collar was produced and a small stock of ties.

"You'd wear a necktie—wouldn't you?" Ross asked, spreading them upon the bureau-top.

"Yes. But make it fall carelessly over your shirt-front," advised the student of *Hints and Helps*. "Your collar is miles too big for me. Say! I've got a wad of white chewing-gum; would you flat it out and stick it over the collar button? Maybe that would fill up some. You kick my foot if you see me turning my head so's to knock it off."

"Better button up your vest," cautioned Ross, laboring with the "careless" fall of his tie.

"Huh-uh! I want 'that easy air which presupposes familiarity with society'—that's what it says in my book," objected Abner.

"Sure!" Ross returned to his more familiar jeering attitude. "Loosen up all your clothes, then. Why don't you untie your shoes? Flop a sock down over one of 'em—that looks 'easy' all right."

Abner buttoned his vest. "It gives a man lots of confidence to know he's good-looking," he remarked, taking all the room in front of the mirror.

Ross, at the wash-stand soaking his hair to get the curl out of it, grumbled some unintelligible response. The two boys went down the stairs with tremulous hearts.

"Why, you've put on another clean shirt, Rossie!" Mrs. Pryor called from her chair—mothers' eyes can see so far! "Well—don't get into any dirty play and soil it." The boys walked in silence—but it was a pregnant silence; for as the roof of the Claiborne house began to peer above the crest of the hill, Ross plumped down on a stone and announced, "I ain't goin'."

"Come on," urged the black-eyed boy. "It'll be fun—and everybody will respect us more. Champe won't throw rocks at us in recess-time, after we've called on her. She couldn't."

"Called!" grunted Ross. "I couldn't make a call any more than a cow. What'd I say? What'd I do? I can behave all right when you just go to people's houses—but a call!"

Abner hesitated. Should he give away his brilliant inside information, drawn from the *Hints and Helps* book, and be rivalled in the glory of his manners and bearing? Why should he not pass on alone, perfectly composed, and reap the field of glory unsupported? His knees gave way and he sat down without intending it.

"Don't you tell anybody and I'll put you on to exactly what grown-up gentlemen say and do when they go calling on the girls," he began.

"Fire away," retorted Ross, gloomily. "Nobody will find out from me. Dead men tell no tales. If I'm fool enough to go, I don't expect to come out of it alive."

Abner rose, white and shaking, and thrusting three fingers into the buttoning of his vest, extending the other hand like an orator, proceeded to instruct the freckled, perspiring disciple at his feet.

"'Hang your hat on the rack, or give it to a servant.'" Ross nodded intelligently. He could do that.

"'Let your legs be gracefully disposed, one hand on the knee, the other — '"

Abner came to an unhappy pause. "I forget what a fellow does with the other hand. Might stick it in your pocket, loudly, or expectorate on the carpet. Indulge in little frivolity. Let a rich stream of conversation flow.'"

Ross mentally dug within himself for sources of rich streams of conversation. He found a dry soil. "What you goin' to talk about?" he demanded, fretfully. "I won't go a step farther till I know what I'm goin' to say when I get there."

Abner began to repeat paragraphs from *Hints and Helps*. "'It is best to remark,'" he opened, in an unnatural voice, "'How well you are looking!' although fulsome compliments should be avoided. When seated ask the young lady who her favorite composer is.'"

"What's a composer?" inquired Ross, with visions of soothing-syrup in his mind.

"A man that makes up music. Don't butt in that way; you put me all out—'composer is. Name yours. Ask her what piece of music she likes best. Name yours. If the lady is musical, here ask her to play or sing.'"

This chanted recitation seemed to have a hypnotic effect on the freckled boy; his big pupils contracted each time Abner came to the repetend, "Name yours."

"I'm tired already," he grumbled; but some spell made him rise and fare farther.

When they had entered the Claiborne gate, they leaned toward each other like young saplings weakened at the root and locking branches to keep what shallow foothold on earth remained.

"You're goin' in first," asserted Ross, but without conviction. It was his custom to tear up to this house a dozen times a week, on his father's old horse or afoot; he was wont to yell for Champe as he approached, and quarrel joyously with her while he performed such errand as he had come upon; but he was gagged and hamstrung now by the hypnotism of Abner's scheme.

"'Walk quietly up the steps; ring the bell and lay your card on the servant,'" quoted Abner, who had never heard of a server.

"'Lay your card on the servant!'" echoed Ross. "Cady'd dodge. There's a porch to cross after you go up the steps — does it say anything about that?"

"It says that the card should be placed on the servant," Abner
reiterated, doggedly. "If Cady dodges, it ain't any business of mine.
There are no porches in my book. Just walk across it like anybody.
We'll ask for Miss Champe Claiborne."

"We haven't got any cards," discovered Ross, with hope.

"I have," announced Abner, pompously. "I had some struck off in
Chicago. I ordered 'em by mail. They got my name Pillow, but there's a
scalloped gilt border around it. You can write your name on my card.
Got a pencil?"

He produced the bit of cardboard; Ross fished up a chewed stump of lead pencil, took it in cold, stiff fingers, and disfigured the square with eccentric scribblings.

"They'll know who it's meant for," he said, apologetically, "because

I'm here. What's likely to happen after we get rid of the card?"

"I told you about hanging your hat on the rack and disposing your legs."

"I remember now," sighed Ross. They had been going slower and slower. The angle of inclination toward each other became more and more pronounced.

"We must stand by each other," whispered Abner.

"I will—if I can stand at all," murmured the other boy, huskily.

"Oh, Lord!" They had rounded the big clump of evergreens and found Aunt Missouri Claiborne placidly rocking on the front porch! Directed to mount steps and ring bell, to lay cards upon the servant, how should one deal with a rosy-faced, plump lady of uncertain years in a rocking-chair. What should a caller lay upon her? A lion in the way could not have been more terrifying. Even retreat was cut off. Aunt Missouri had seen them. "Howdy, boys; how are you?" she said, rocking peacefully. The two stood before her like detected criminals.

Then, to Ross's dismay, Abner sank down on the lowest step of the porch, the westering sun full in his hopeless eyes. He sat on his cap. It was characteristic that the freckled boy remained standing. He would walk up those steps according to plan and agreement, if at all. He accepted no compromise. Folding his straw hat into a battered cone, he watched anxiously for the delivery of the card. He was not sure what Aunt Missouri's attitude might be if it were laid on her. He bent down to his companion. "Go ahead," he whispered. "Lay the card."

Abner raised appealing eyes. "In a minute. Give me time," he pleaded.

"Mars' Ross—Mars' Ross! Head 'em off!" sounded a yell, and Babe, the house-boy, came around the porch in pursuit of two half-grown chickens.

"Help him, Rossie," prompted Aunt Missouri, sharply. "You boys can stay to supper and have some of the chicken if you help catch them."

Had Ross taken time to think, he might have reflected that gentlemen making formal calls seldom join in a chase after the main dish of the family supper. But the needs of Babe were instant. The lad flung himself sidewise, caught one chicken in his hat, while Babe fell upon the other in the manner of a football player. Ross handed the pullet to the house-boy, fearing that he had done something very much out of character, then pulled the reluctant negro toward to the steps.

"Babe's a servant," he whispered to Abner, who had sat rigid through the entire performance. "I helped him with the chickens, and he's got to stand gentle while you lay the card on."

Confronted by the act itself, Abner was suddenly aware that he knew not how to begin. He took refuge in dissimulation.

"Hush!" he whispered back. "Don't you see Mr. Claiborne's come out? — He's going to read something to us."

Ross plumped down beside him. "Never mind the card; tell 'em," he urged.

"Tell 'em yourself."

"No — let's cut and run."

"I — I think the worst of it is over. When Champe sees us she'll — "

Mention of Champe stiffened Ross's spine. If it had been glorious to call upon her, how very terrible she would make it should they attempt calling, fail, and the failure come to her knowledge! Some things were easier to endure than others; he resolved to stay till the call was made.

For half an hour the boys sat with drooping heads, and the old gentleman read aloud, presumably to Aunt Missouri and themselves. Finally their restless eyes discerned the two Claiborne girls walking serene in Sunday trim under the trees at the edge of the lawn. Arms entwined, they were whispering together and giggling a little. A caller, Ross dared not use his voice to shout nor his legs to run toward them.

"Why don't you go and talk to the girls, Rossie?" Aunt Missouri asked, in the kindness of her heart. "Don't be noisy — it's Sunday, you know — and don't get to playing anything that'll dirty up your good clothes."

Ross pressed his lips hard together; his heart swelled with the rage of the misunderstood. Had the card been in his possession, he would, at that instant, have laid it on Aunt Missouri without a qualm.

"What is it?" demanded the old gentleman, a bit testily.

"The girls want to hear you read, father," said Aunt Missouri, shrewdly; and she got up and trotted on short, fat ankles to the girls in the arbor. The three returned together, Alicia casting curious glances at the uncomfortable youths, Champe threatening to burst into giggles with every breath.

Abner sat hard on his cap and blushed silently. Ross twisted his hat into a three-cornered wreck.

The two girls settled themselves noisily on the upper step. The old man read on and on. The sun sank lower. The hills were red in the west as though a brush fire flamed behind their crests. Abner stole a furtive glance at his companion in misery, and the dolor of Ross's countenance somewhat assuaged his anguish. The freckle-faced boy was thinking of the village over the hill, a certain pleasant white house set back in a green yard, past whose gate, the two-plank sidewalk ran. He knew lamps were beginning to wink in the windows of the neighbors about, as though the houses said, "Our

14

boys are all at home—but Ross Pryor's out trying to call on the girls, and can't get anybody to understand it." Oh, that he were walking down those two planks, drawing a stick across the pickets, lifting high happy feet which could turn in at that gate! He wouldn't care what the lamps said then. He wouldn't even mind if the whole Claiborne family died laughing at him—if only some power would raise him up from this paralyzing spot and put him behind the safe barriers of his own home!

The old man's voice lapsed into silence; the light was becoming too dim for his reading. Aunt Missouri turned and called over her shoulder into the shadows of the big hall: "You Babe! Go put two extra plates on the supper-table."

The boys grew red from the tips of their ears, and as far as any one could see under their wilting collars. Abner felt the lump of gum come loose and slip down a cold spine. Had their intentions but been known, this inferential invitation would have been most welcome. It was but to rise up and thunder out, "We came to call on the young ladies."

They did not rise. They did not thunder out anything. Babe brought a lamp and set it inside the window, and Mr. Claiborne resumed his reading. Champe giggled and said that Alicia made her. Alcia drew her skirts about her, sniffed, and looked virtuous, and said she didn't see anything funny to laugh at. The supper-bell rang. The family, evidently taking it for granted that the boys would follow, went in.

Alone for the first time, Abner gave up. "This ain't any use," he complained. "We ain't calling on anybody."

"Why didn't you lay on the card?" demanded Ross, fiercely. "Why didn't you say: 'We've-just-dropped-into-call-on-Miss-Champe. It's-a -pleasant-evening. We-feel-we-must-be-going,' like you said you would? Then we could have lifted our hats and got away decently."

Abner showed no resentment.

"Oh, if it's so easy, why didn't you do it yourself?" he groaned.

"Somebody's coming," Ross muttered, hoarsely. "Say it now. Say it quick."

The somebody proved to be Aunt Missouri, who advanced only as far as the end of the hall and shouted cheerfully: "The idea of a growing boy not coming to meals when the bell rings! I thought you two would be in there ahead of us. Come on." And clinging to their head-coverings as though these contained some charm whereby the owners might be rescued, the unhappy callers were herded into the dining-room. There were many things on the table that boys like. Both were becoming fairly cheerful, when Aunt Missouri checked the biscuit-plate with: "I treat my neighbors' children just like I'd want children of my own treated. If your mothers let you eat all you want, say so, and I don't care; but if either of them is a little bit particular, why, I'd stop at six!"

Still reeling from this blow, the boys finally rose from the table and passed out with the family, their hats clutched to their bosoms, and clinging together for mutual aid and comfort. During the usual Sunday-evening singing Champe laughed till Aunt Missouri threatened to send her to bed. Abner's card slipped from his hand and dropped face up on the floor. He fell upon it and tore it into infinitesimal pieces.

"That must have been a love-letter," said Aunt Missouri, in a pause of the music. "You boys are getting 'most old enough to think about beginning to call on the girls." Her eyes twinkled.

Ross growled like a stoned cur. Abner took a sudden dive into *Hints and Helps*, and came up with, "You flatter us, Miss Claiborne," whereat Ross snickered out like a human boy. They all stared at him.

"It sounds so funny to call Aunt Missouri 'Mis' Claiborne,'" the lad of the freckles explained.

"Funny?" Aunt Missouri reddened. "I don't see any particular joke in my having my maiden name."

Abner, who instantly guessed at what was in Ross's mind, turned white at the thought of what they had escaped. Suppose he had laid on the card and asked for Miss Claiborne!

"What's the matter, Champe?" inquired Ross, in a fairly natural tone. The air he had drawn into his lungs when he laughed at Abner seemed to relieve him from the numbing gentility which had bound his powers since he joined Abner's ranks.

"Nothing. I laughed because you laughed," said the girl.

The singing went forward fitfully. Servants traipsed through the darkened yard, going home for Sunday night. Aunt Missouri went out and held some low-toned parley with them. Champe yawned with insulting enthusiasm. Presently both girls quietly disappeared. Aunt Missouri never returned to the parlor—evidently thinking that the girls would attend to the final amenities with their callers. They were left alone with old Mr. Claiborne. They sat as though bound in their chairs, while the old man read in silence for a while. Finally he closed his book, glanced about him, and observed absently:

"So you boys were to spend the night?" Then, as he looked at their startled faces: "I'm right, am I not? You are to spent the night?"

Oh, for courage to say: "Thank you, no. We'll be going now. We just came over to call on Miss Champe." But thought of how this would sound in face of the facts, the painful realization that they dared not say it because they *had* not said it, locked their lips. Their feet were lead; their tongues stiff and too large for their mouths. Like creatures in a nightmare, they moved stiffly, one might have said creakingly, up the stairs and received each—a bedroom candle!

"Good night, children," said the absent-minded old man. The two gurgled out some sounds which were intended for words and doged behind the bedroom door.

"They've put us to bed!" Abner's black eyes flashed fire. His nervous hands clutched at the collar Ross had lent him. "That's what I get for coming here with you, Ross Pryor!" And tears of humiliation stood in his eyes.

In his turn Ross showed no resentment. "What I'm worried about is my mother," he confessed. "She's so sharp about finding out things. She wouldn't tease me — she'd just be sorry for me. But she'll think I went home with you."

"I'd like to see my mother make a fuss about my calling on the girls!" growled Abner, glad to let his rage take a safe direction.

"Calling on the girls! Have we called on any girls?" demanded clear-headed, honest Ross.

"Not exactly — yet," admitted Abner, reluctantly. "Come on — let's go to bed. Mr. Claiborne asked us, and he's the head of this household. It isn't anybody's business what we came for."

"I'll slip off my shoes and lie down till Babe ties up the dog in the morning," said Ross. "Then we can get away before any of the family is up."

Oh, youth — youth — youth, with its rash promises! Worn out with misery the boys slept heavily. The first sound that either heard in the morning was Babe hammering upon their bedroom door. They crouched guiltily and looked into each other's eyes. "Let pretend we ain't here and he'll go away," breathed Abner.

But Babe was made of sterner stuff. He rattled the knob. He   turned   it. He put in a black face with a grin which divided it from ear   to   ear. "Cady say I mus' call dem fool boys to breakfus'," he announced.   "I never named you-all dat. Cady, she say dat."

"Breakfast!" echoed Ross, in a daze.

"Yessuh, breakfus'," reasserted Babe, coming entirely into the room and looking curiously about him. "Ain't you-all done been to bed at all?" wrapping his arms about his shoulders and shaking with silent ecstasies of mirth. The boys threw themselves upon him and ejected him.

"Sent up a servant to call us to breakfast," snarled Abner. "If they'd only sent their old servant to the door in the first place, all this wouldn't 'a' happened. I'm just that way when I get thrown off the track. You know how it was when I tried to repeat those things to you—I had to go clear back to the beginning when I got interrupted."

"Does that mean that you're still hanging around here to begin over and make a call?" asked Ross, darkly. "I won't go down to breakfast if you are."

Abner brightened a little as he saw Ross becoming wordy in his rage. "I dare you to walk downstairs and say, 'We-just-dropped-in-to-call-on-Miss-Champe'!" he said.

"I—oh—I—darn it all! there goes the second bell. We may as well trot down."

"Don't leave me, Ross," pleaded the Jilton boy. "I can't stay here—and I can't go down."

The tone was hysterical. The boy with freckles took his companion by the arm without another word and marched him down the stairs. "We may get a chance yet to call on Champe all by herself out on the porch or in the arbor before she goes to school," he suggested, by way of putting some spine into the black-eyed boy.

An emphatic bell rang when they were half-way down the stairs. Clutching their hats, they slunk into the dining-room. Even Mr. Claiborne seemed to notice something unusual in their bearing as they settled into the chairs assigned to them, and asked them kindly if they had slept well.

It was plain that Aunt Missouri had been posting him as to her understanding of the intentions of these young men. The state of affairs gave an electric hilarity to the atmosphere. Babe travelled from the sideboard to the table, trembling like chocolate pudding. Cady insisted on bringing in the cakes herself, and grinned as she whisked her starched blue skirts in and out of the dining-room. A dimple even showed itself at the corners

21

of pretty Alicia's prim little mouth. Champe giggled, till Ross heard Cady whisper:

"Now you got one dem snickerin' spells agin. You gwine bust yo' dress buttons off in the back ef you don't mind."

As the spirits of those about them mounted, the hearts of the two youths sank—if it was like this among the Claibornes, what would it be at school and in the world at large when their failure to connect intention with result became village talk? Ross bit fiercely upon an unoffending batter-cake, and resolved to make a call single-handed before he left the house.

They went out of the dining-room, their hats as ever pressed to their breasts. With no volition of their own, their uncertain young legs carried them to the porch. The Claiborne family and household followed like small boys after a circus procession. When the two turned, at bay, yet with nothing between them and liberty but a hypnotism of their own suggestion, they saw the black faces of the servants peering over the family shoulders.

Ross was the boy to have drawn courage from the desperation of their case, and made some decent if not glorious ending. But at the psychological moment there came around the corner of the house that most contemptible figure known to the Southern plantation, a shirt-boy—a creature who may be described, for the benefit of those not informed, as a pickaninny clad only in a long, coarse cotton shirt. While all eyes were fastened upon him this inglorious ambassador bolted forth his message:

"Yo' ma say"—his eyes were fixed upon Abner—"ef yo' don' come home, she gwine come after yo'—an' cut yo' into inch pieces wid a rawhide when she git yo'. Dat jest what Miss Hortense say."

As though such a book as *Hints and Helps* had never existed, Abner shot for the gate—he was but a hobbledehoy fascinated with the idea of playing gentleman. But in Ross there were the makings of a man. For a few half-hearted paces, under the first impulse of horror, he followed his deserting chief, the laughter of the family, the unrestrainable guffaws of the negroes, sounding in the rear. But when Champe's high, offensive giggle, topping all the others, insulted his ears, he stopped dead, wheeled, and ran to the porch faster than he had fled from it. White as paper, shaking with inexpressible rage, he caught and kissed the tittering girl, violently, noisily, before them all.

The negroes fled—they dared not trust their feelings; even Alicia sniggered unobtrusively; Grandfather Claiborne chuckled, and Aunt Missouri frankly collapsed into her rocking-chair, bubbling with mirth, crying out:

"Good for you, Ross! Seems you did know how to call on the girls, after all."

But Ross, paying no attention, walked swiftly toward the gate. He had served his novitiate. He would never be afraid again. With cheerful alacrity he dodged the stones flung after him with friendly, erratic aim by the girl upon whom, yesterday afternoon, he had come to make a social call.

End of the Book

www.ingramcontent.com/pod-product-compliance
Lightning Source LLC
Chambersburg PA
CBHW060022300526

45794CB00003B/1258